The Nature Kid's Guide to
DOLPHINS

RENATA MARIE

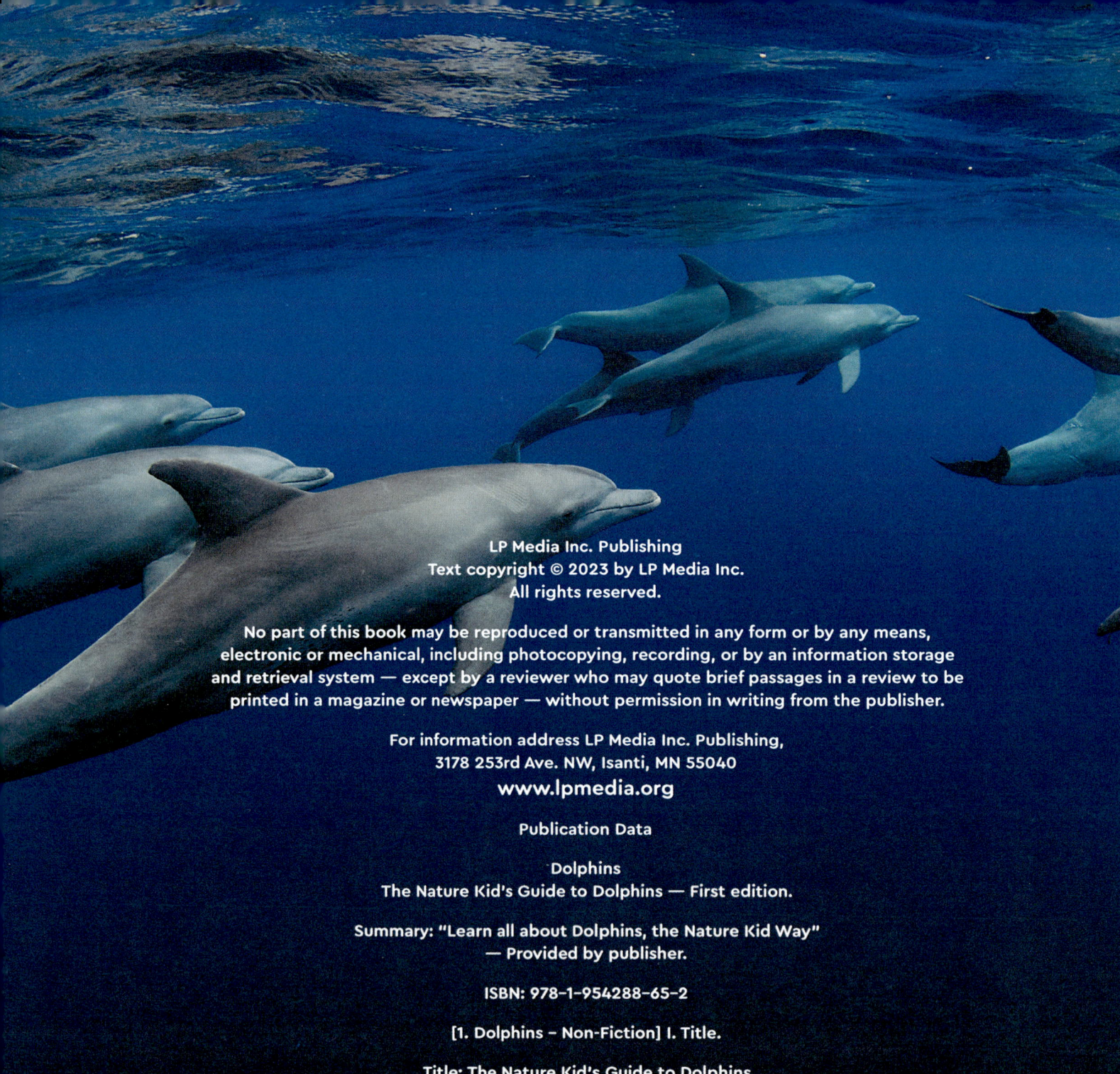

LP Media Inc. Publishing
Text copyright © 2023 by LP Media Inc.
All rights reserved.

No part of this book may be reproduced or transmitted in any form or by any means, electronic or mechanical, including photocopying, recording, or by an information storage and retrieval system — except by a reviewer who may quote brief passages in a review to be printed in a magazine or newspaper — without permission in writing from the publisher.

For information address LP Media Inc. Publishing,
3178 253rd Ave. NW, Isanti, MN 55040
www.lpmedia.org

Publication Data

Dolphins
The Nature Kid's Guide to Dolphins — First edition.

Summary: "Learn all about Dolphins, the Nature Kid Way"
— Provided by publisher.

ISBN: 978-1-954288-65-2

[1. Dolphins – Non-Fiction] I. Title.

Title: The Nature Kid's Guide to Dolphins

CONTENTS

Jump In! 4

Strong Swimmers 6

Sharp Eyes 8

Super Sounds 10

Smart Hunters 12

Fishy Treats 14

Fin in the Water 16

Big Brains 18

Best Friends 20

Sleep-Swimming 22

First Breath 24

A Perfect Wave 26

Mother and Teacher 28

Musical Voices 30

Too Many People 32

Noisy Neighbors 34

Netted 36

Swimming in Circles 38

JUMP IN!

Splash! **A bottlenose dolphin jumps. He dives. He whistles and clicks.**

Dolphins live in the ocean. Some live close to the shore. Others live in the open ocean.

They play in waves. They hunt with bubbles. And they send whistles through the water. These friendly animals are ready to make a big splash!

FUN FACT!

There are 36 types of dolphins. Most live in the ocean, but a few live in rivers.

STRONG SWIMMERS

13 FEET   10 FEET   6 FEET

A dolphin's strong tail pushes him through the water.

Dolphin bodies are long and strong. Their skin is smooth. They move easily through the water. Their top fin keeps them steady. Their side fins help them change direction.

Male dolphins can be 13 feet (4.0 meters) long and can weigh over 1,000 pounds (454 kilograms). Female dolphins are usually smaller than males.

FUN FACT! Bottlenose dolphins get their name from their bottle-shaped noses.

SHARP EYES

A dolphin is hungry.
She looks for tasty fish.

Dolphins have sharp eyes. They can see well in the water. They can see well out of the water. One eye can look to the side while the other looks ahead. They can look back. When they spot food, they take off.

DID YOU KNOW?

Dolphins breathe air. They breathe out of a hole on top of their heads. It is called a blowhole. They can hold their breath for about 10 minutes.

SUPER SOUNDS

Click ... Click ... A dolphin clicks to find fish.

Dolphins use **echolocation** to find food. **They send sound out into the water.** The sound hits a fish. It comes back. Dolphins have strong hearing. The sound travels through their mouths to their ears.

The sound tells them how big the fish is. They know its shape. They know how fast it is swimming. And they know where the fish is.

FUN FACT!

Dolphins also use echolocation to stay away from predators like sharks.

SMART HUNTERS

DID YOU KNOW? Dolphins have up to 100 teeth.

Fish dart. They dive. But they cannot escape. The dolphins are everywhere.

Dolphins work together to catch food. They blow bubbles to push the fish up. They slap their tails. They make a lot of clicks. **They circle the fish.** The fish get close together. Then, the dolphins charge. Dolphins can swim up to 20 miles (32 kilometers) per hour.

Dolphins also use the shore to catch food. They rush at the fish. The fish swim toward land. They are trapped, and the dolphins easily catch them.

FISHY TREATS

FUN FACT!
Dolphins do not chew their food. They swallow it whole.

An Amazon river dolphin swallows a fish, but he is still hungry.

Dolphins are **carnivores**. **They eat meat.** Dolphins eat fish. They eat squid and shrimp. They eat crabs and octopuses. They even eat jellyfish and eels. Dolphins can eat up to 30 pounds (14 kg) a day.

Fish   Eel   Jellyfish   Squid

FIN IN THE WATER

Bull Shark

Great White Shark

Killer Whale

Tiger Shark

A fin cuts through the water, but it is not a dolphin.

Dolphins are top **predators**. Few animals hunt them, but some hunters are bigger.

Dolphins have to watch out for killer whales and sharks. They are safe if they stay in a large group. If a shark charges, they fight back. They chase it. They bite it. They ram it with their noses. They keep their young, old, and sick dolphins safe.

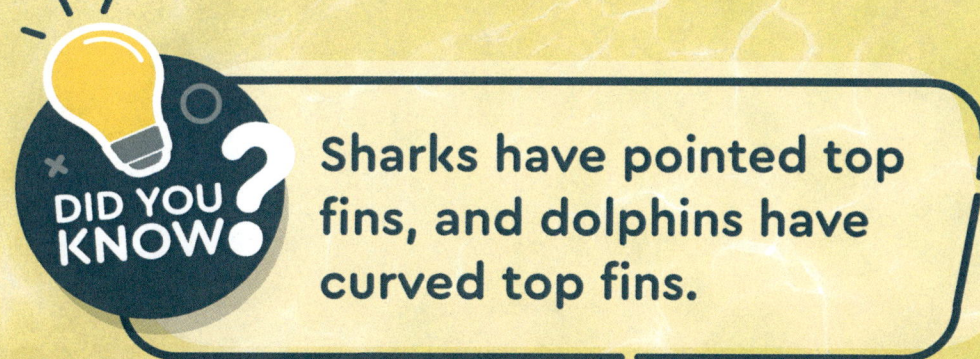

DID YOU KNOW? Sharks have pointed top fins, and dolphins have curved top fins.

BIG BRAINS

FUN FACT!

Each dolphin has a name. It sounds like a whistle. Other dolphins use this whistle to call it.

Little fish hide in the sand, but a dolphin learned a trick from her friend.

Dolphins are one of the smartest animals on Earth. They push fish out of the sand with their noses. They use soft sponges to keep their noses safe. They use shells to lift fish out of the water and swallow them. They can look in a **mirror** and see it is them and not another dolphin. They learn tricks from other dolphins. They even learn how to whistle like humans.

***Squeak!* A dolphin spots his friend. It has been a long time.**

Dolphins move to different parts of the ocean. They go where there is food. They go where it is warm. Sometimes, they run into dolphins they met before. **They can remember a friend for up to 20 years.** That is a long time for animals!

FUN FACT! Dolphins can swim up to 100 miles (161 km) a day.

SLEEP-SWIMMING

Swimming all day is tiring. A dolphin takes a nap, but part of it is still awake.

A group of dolphins floats at the top of the water. They are sleeping. But they still stick together. How do they do this?

Dolphins sleep with half of their brain at a time. One half sleeps. One half stays awake. They keep one eye open. They stay close together. They watch for predators. They keep each other safe.

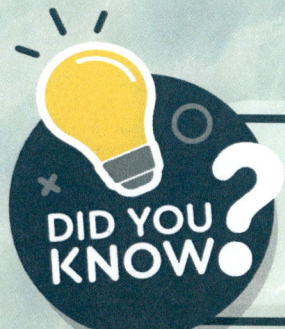

DID YOU KNOW? Killer whales are not whales. They are a type of dolphin.

FIRST BREATH

A young dolphin takes his first breath.

Dolphin babies are called calves. When a calf is born, its mother lifts it to the air. It takes its first breath.

Calves swim next to their mothers. Here, they can easily drink milk and it is easier to swim. Their fins are not hard yet. The mother pushes most of the water away. Then the calf can keep up with the group.

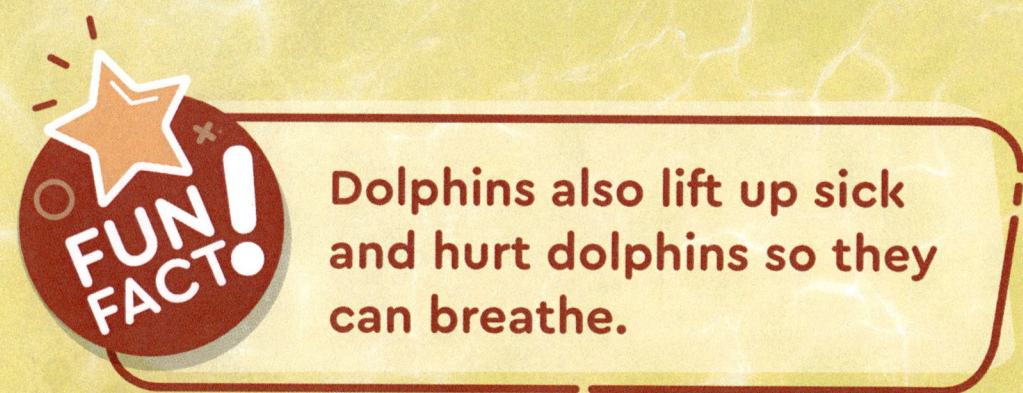

Dolphins also lift up sick and hurt dolphins so they can breathe.

A PERFECT WAVE

The calf jumps. He rolls with his friends.

A group of dolphins is called a pod.
Dolphins like to live together. They hunt together. They keep each other safe. They make friends.

Dolphins play together. They make bubble rings and swim through them. They ride waves behind boats.

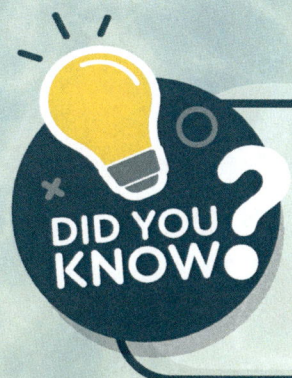

DID YOU KNOW? Pods usually have up to 30 dolphins, but there can be hundreds of dolphins in a pod.

MOTHER AND TEACHER

The calf learns to use shells. He learns to catch fish.

Calves stay with their mothers for three to six years. At 18 months, they stop drinking milk. They learn how to hunt. They learn how to talk to other dolphins. They learn how to watch out for predators.

Then they leave. They find their own pods to call home.

An "auntie" dolphin sometimes helps raise the calf.

MUSICAL VOICES

Sounds flow through the water. They sound like music.

A pod of dolphins clicks and whistles to each other. They squawk and squeak. They bark and yelp. They trill and grunt. They moan and groan.

Dolphins also use their bodies to talk. They jump into the air. They snap their mouths. They slap their tails. They blow **bubbles**. They bump each other.

FUN FACT!

Dolphins can jump 20 feet (6.1 m) into the air.

TOO MANY PEOPLE

A dolphin jumps near the beach. He shakes his head. A plastic bag falls off his nose.

Humans built buildings by the shore. They crowded the beaches. They left their waste on the sand. It blew into the ocean. **Trash can make dolphins sick.** It can make it hard to swim.

Most types of dolphins are not in danger of dying out, but they still have to watch out for people, waste, nets, and boats.

DID YOU KNOW? Five types of dolphins are endangered. Some are river dolphins. Others live in the ocean. Nowhere is safe.

NOISY NEIGHBORS

34

A boat screams by the beach. It makes it hard for dolphins to hear.

People drive boats by the beach. They might hit dolphins or cut them. **People make sounds with machines.** It fills the ocean. Dolphins cannot hear. They cannot find each other. They cannot find food.

DID YOU KNOW? What do you do if you see a dolphin on the beach? Stay away. Tell an adult. Dolphins end up on beaches when they are hurt or sick. Putting a dolphin back in the water could hurt it more.

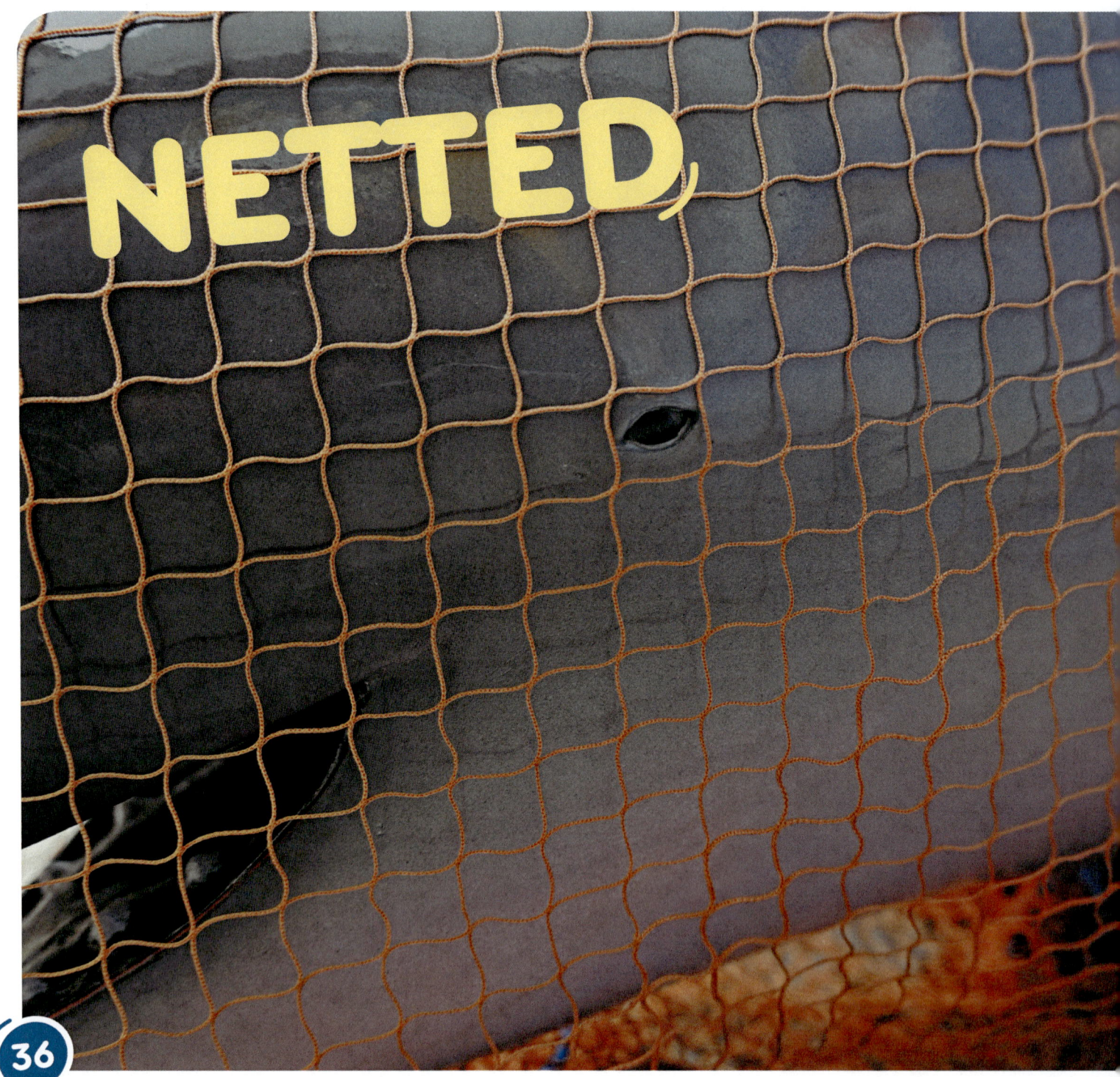
NETTED,

A net falls over a dolphin. She tries to swim, but she is trapped.

People use big fishing nets to catch fish. **Sometimes they catch other animals too.** Dolphins can get trapped in nets. They cannot swim up to breathe.

People are trying to help dolphins. They send out noises from fishing boats. The noises tell dolphins to stay away. If people see a dolphin in a net, they cut it free.

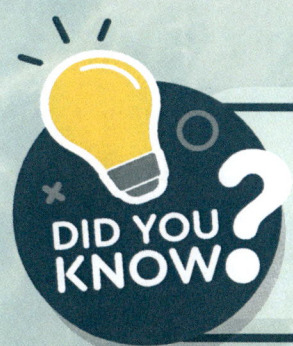

DID YOU KNOW? Dolphins can sometimes save people from aggressive sharks.

Circle ... Circle ... Circle ...

Dolphins are safe from predators in tanks. **But tanks are too small for dolphins.** Swimming in circles all day hurts their brains. They are too smart.

Dolphins need space to play. They need fish to hunt. They need to be part of a family.

Zoos help some animals. But dolphins are meant to jump, splash, and be free.

FUN FACT! Dolphins live for 40 to 50 years. Some even live for 60 years.

GLOSSARY

carnivores
animals that eat meat
page 15

echolocation
using sound
to find things
page 11

endangered
in danger
page 33

mirror
an object a person or an animal can see themself in
page 19

predators
animals that hunt
other animals
page 17

whistles
to make a high sound
page 5

MORE AMAZING ANIMAL BOOKS
from Nature Kids Publishing!

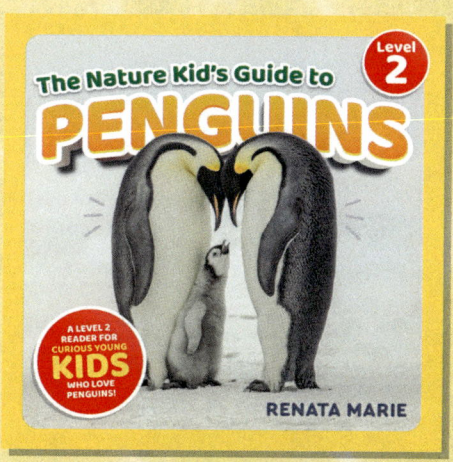
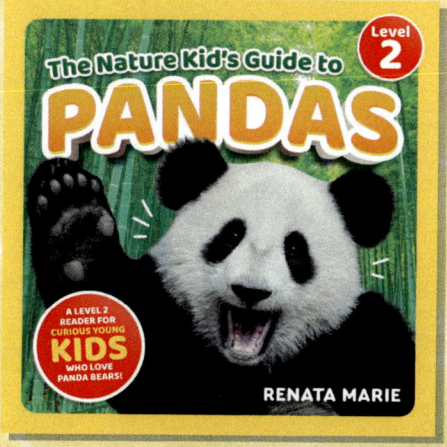

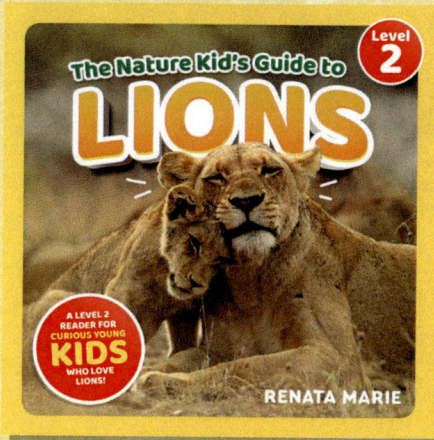

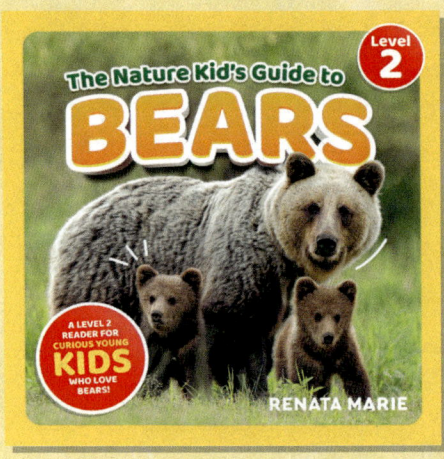

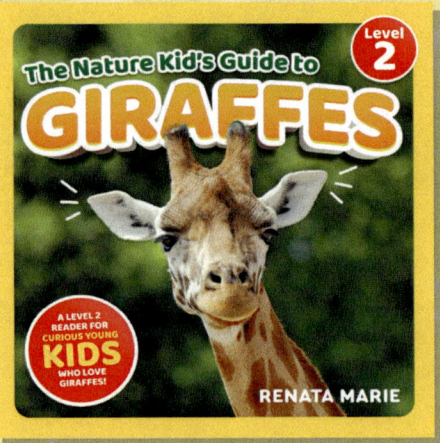

Visit NatureKidsPublishing.com to Learn More!

Made in the USA
Las Vegas, NV
28 March 2024